Rain Forest Experiments

10 Science Experiments in One Hour or Less

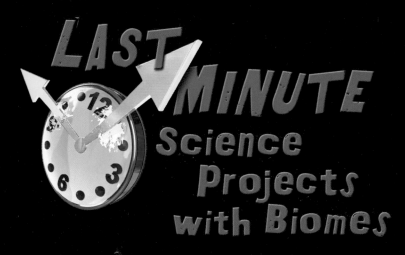

LAST MINUTE Science Projects with Biomes

ROBERT GARDNER
ILLUSTRATED BY TOM LABAFF

Enslow Publishers, Inc.
40 Industrial Road
Box 398
Berkeley Heights, NJ 07922
USA

http://www.enslow.com

Library of Congress Cataloging-in-Publication Data:

Gardner, Robert, 1929– author.
    Rain forest experiments : 10 science experiments in one hour or less / Robert Gardner.
        pages cm. — (Last minute science projects with biomes)
    Summary: "A variety of science projects that can be done in under an hour, plus a few that take longer for
        interested students"— Provided by publisher.
    Includes bibliographical references and index.
    ISBN 978-0-7660-5937-5
    1. Rain forest ecology—Experiments—Juvenile literature. 2. Rain forests—Experiments—Juvenile
        literature. 3. Science projects—Juvenile literature. I. Title.
    QH541.5.R27G367 2014
    577.34'078—dc23

                                    2013014027

Future editions:
Paperback ISBN: 978-0-7660-5938-2
EPUB ISBN: 978-0-7660-5939-9
Single-User PDF ISBN: 978-0-7660-5940-5
Multi-User PDF ISBN: 978-0-7660-5941-2

Printed in the United States of America

052014 Lake Book Manufacturing, Inc., Melrose Park, IL

10 9 8 7 6 5 4 3 2 1

To Our Readers: We have done our best to make sure all Internet Addresses in this book were active and appropriate when we went to press. However, the author and the publisher have no control over and assume no liability for the material available on those Internet sites or on other Web sites they may link to. Any comments or suggestions can be sent by e-mail to comments@enslow.com or to the address on the back cover.

♻ Enslow Publishers, Inc., is committed to printing our books on recycled paper. The paper in every book contains 10% to 30% post-consumer waste (PCW). The cover board on the outside of each book contains 100% PCW. Our goal is to do our part to help young people and the environment too!

Illustration Credits: Tom LaBaff (www.tomlabaff.com)

Photo Credits: ©1999 Artville, LLC; Nicholas Bergkessel, Jr./Science Source, p. 18(flying squirrel); Shutterstock.com: ©CHAINFOTO24, p. 5, ©TranceDrumer, p. 7(Blue Morpho butterfly), ©Waraphan Rattanawong, p. 7 (Hercules beetle), ©Hugh Lansdown, p. 16, ©alslutsky, p. 23, ©think4photop, p. 29, ©hallam creations, p. 35(top), Stephen Dalton/Science Source, p. 18(frog), ©Thinkstock: Alfredo Maiquez/ iStock, p. 6, Andrea Danti/Hemera, p. 43, ©Geraldass/iStock, p. 24, ©Lauren Darcey/Hemera, p. 35 (grassland hippo), nkuzmina/iStock , p. 7(sloth), Victor Soares/Hemera, p. 7 (macaws)

Cover Photos: Shutterstock.com: ©Onur YILDIRIM (clock with yellow arrows); ©Videowokart (house plant), ©dinodentist(random leaves), ©Thinkstock/istock: furtaev (main figure), James Trice (toothpicks)

Contents

LAST MINUTE Science Projects with Biomes

🎖 Indicates an experiment that features an idea for a science fair or project

An Introduction to Rain Forest Experiments

If you have a science project that is due soon, maybe tomorrow, this book will help you. It has experiments about tropical rain forests. Many of the experiments can be done in less than one hour. An estimate of the time needed is given for each experiment. Perhaps you have plenty of time to prepare for your next science project or fair. You can still use and enjoy this book.

Many experiments are followed by a "Keep Exploring" section. There you will find ideas for more science projects. The details are left to you, the young scientist. You can design and carry out your own experiments, **under adult supervision**, when you have more time.

For some experiments, you may need a partner to help you. Work with someone who likes to do experiments as much as you do. Then you will both enjoy what you are doing. In this book, if any safety issues or danger is involved in doing an experiment, you will be warned. **In some cases you will be asked to work with an adult. Please do so.** Don't take any chances that could lead to an injury.

Rain Forest Biomes

A biome is a region of the earth with a particular climate. The plants and animals that live in a biome are quite similar all around the world. This book is about rain forests. But there are other biomes. Earth's land biomes include deserts, tundra, taiga, grasslands, tropical rain forests, and temperate forests.

A tropical rain forest is a warm, humid place. The average annual temperature is about 27°C (81°F). As its name indicates, there is a lot of rain—at least 180 cm (70 inches) and as much as 635 cm (250 inches) per year.

Rain forests cover approximately seven percent of Earth's land. They are located between the Tropic of Cancer and the Tropic of Capricorn. So they lie within 23.5 degrees latitude north or south of the equator. Their location means this biome has only one season—summer. If you like warm, humid weather, you might enjoy living in a rain forest.

The emergent, or top, layer of a rain forest consists of evergreen trees 40 to 76 meters (130 to 250 feet) tall. The top branches of one of these trees may cover an acre (43,560 square feet or 4,049 square meters). The second layer is the canopy. It has trees 20 to 40 meters (65 to 130 feet) in height. These trees cover the rest of the forest. Only about two percent of the sunlight striking the forest gets through the canopy. As a result, the shorter trees and plants that make up the understory must be adapted to dim light to survive. Many rain forest plants, such as orchids and bromeliads, are epiphytes. They grow on trees and other plants rather than rooting in soil.

Rain forests contain more living species than any other biome. The top layer of the rain forest is called the canopy.

Epiphytes are plants that grow on plants and trees, not rooted in soil.

Rain forests contain more living species than any other biome. A typical plot of rain forest 3.2 kilometers (2 miles) on a side is likely to contain 750 kinds of trees and an equal number of other plant species. In the same area you may find more than 100 species of mammals and reptiles, 400 bird species, and 60 species of amphibians. But even more abundant are insects and other arthropods, which make up the vast majority of species in the rain forest (and on the earth!).

A rich variety of life is not accompanied by rich soil. These forest soils lack a high concentration of nutrients. The reason is that the plants absorb the nutrients rapidly. Consequently, the nutrients are found in the plants, not the soil.

Sadly, rain forests are disappearing at a rapid rate. Each year, large areas of rain forests are cleared and burned in Brazil, Indonesia, and other countries. Approximately 12 million hectares (30 million acres) of rain forests are destroyed each year. Such clearing also adds to global warming. Through photosynthesis, the trees remove carbon dioxide (a greenhouse gas) from the atmosphere while adding huge volumes of oxygen.

Rain forests contain half of the earth's known species, as well as more than 350 different ethnic groups of humans. Seventy percent of the plants that have known medicinal value are found here. So the destruction of rain forests hinders medical progress.

When rain forests are cleared, the shallow soil is exposed to heavy rains. The rains carry the soil away because there is no vegetation to hold it in place. As Table 1 reveals, deforestation, mostly the destruction of rain forests, added 5.43 billion tons of carbon dioxide to Earth's air.

If the trees had been allowed to live, 5.43 billion tons of carbon dioxide would have been removed from the air.

Table 1: Major additions of carbon dioxide to the world's air in 2008 (billions of tons).	
China 6.89	European Union 5.07
USA 6.73	India 2.24
Deforestation (worldwide) 5.43	

Clockwise from top left: macaws, two-toed sloth, morpho butterfly, and Hercules tree beetle

The Scientific Method

To do experiments the way scientists do, you need to know about the scientific method. It is true that scientists in different areas of science use different ways of experimenting. Depending on the problem, one method is likely to be better than another. Designing a new medicine for heart disease and finding evidence of water on Mars require different kinds of experiments.

Despite these differences, all scientists use a similar approach as they experiment. It is called the scientific method. In most experimenting, some or all of the following steps are used: making an observation, coming up with a question, creating a hypothesis (a possible answer to the question) and a prediction (an if-then statement), designing and conducting an experiment, analyzing results, drawing conclusions about the prediction, and deciding if the hypothesis is true or false. Scientists share the results of their experiments by writing articles that are published in science journals.

You might wonder how you can use the scientific method. You begin when you see, read, or hear about something in the world that makes you curious. So you ask a question. To find an answer, you do a well-designed investigation; you use the scientific method.

Once you have a question, you can make a hypothesis. Your hypothesis is a possible answer to the question (what you think is true). For example, you might hypothesize that rainfall is the same in all kinds of forest. Once you have a hypothesis, it is time to design an experiment to test your hypothesis.

In most cases, you should do a controlled experiment. This means having two subjects that are treated the same except for the one thing being tested. That thing is called a variable. For example, to test the hypothesis above, you might measure the annual rainfall in a taiga, temperate forest, and rain forest during the course of a decade. You would find that the rainfall in the rain forest is significantly greater than in the other forests. You would have to conclude that your hypothesis was incorrect.

The results of one experiment often lead to another question. In the case above, that experiment might lead you to ask, what effect does less rainfall have on the kind of plants and animals we find in a forest? Whatever the results, something can be learned from every experiment!

Science Fairs

Some of the investigations in this book contain ideas that might be used as a science fair project. Those ideas are indicated with a symbol (). However, judges at science fairs do not reward projects or experiments that are simply copied from a book. For example, a diagram of a leaf of grass would not impress most judges. However, an experiment that measured the effect of rainfall on the growth rate of grass would attract their attention.

Science fair judges tend to reward creative thought and imagination. It is difficult to be creative or imaginative unless you are really interested in your project. Therefore, try to choose something that excites you. And before you jump into a project, consider, too, your own talents and the cost of the materials you will need.

If you decide to use an experiment or idea found in this book as a science fair project, find ways to modify or extend it. This should not be difficult. As you do investigations, new ideas will come to mind. You will think of questions that experiments can answer. The experiments will make excellent science fair projects, especially because the ideas are yours and are interesting to you.

Safety First

Safety is very important in science. Certain rules should be followed when doing experiments. Some of the rules below may seem obvious to you, others may not, but it is important that you follow all of them.

1. Do any experiments or projects, whether from this book or of your own design, under the supervision of a science teacher or other knowledgeable adult.

2. Read all instructions carefully before proceeding with a project. If you have questions, check with your supervisor before going further.

3. Always wear safety goggles when doing experiments that could cause particles to enter your eyes. Tie back long hair and do not wear open-toed shoes.

4. Do not eat or drink while experimenting. Never taste substances being used (unless instructed to do so).

5. Do not touch chemicals.

6. Do not let water drops fall on a hot lightbulb.

7. The liquid in some older thermometers is mercury (a dense liquid metal). It is dangerous to touch mercury or breathe its vapor. That is why mercury thermometers have been banned in many states. When doing experiments, use only non-mercury thermometers, such as digital thermometers or those filled with alcohol. If you have a mercury thermometer in the house, ask an adult to take it to a place where it can be exchanged or safely discarded.

8. Do only those experiments that are described in the book or those that have been approved by an adult.

9. Maintain a serious attitude while conducting experiments. Never engage in horseplay or play practical jokes.

10. Remove all items not needed for the experiment from your work space.

11. At the end of every activity, clean all materials used and put them away. Then wash your hands thoroughly with soap and water

A Note About Your Notebook

Your notebook, as any scientist will tell you, is a valuable possession. It should contain ideas you may have as you experiment, sketches you draw, calculations you make, and hypotheses you suggest. It should include a description of every experiment you do; the data you record, such as volumes, temperatures, masses; and so on. It should also contain the results of your experiments, graphs you draw, and any conclusions you make based on your results.

20 Minutes or Less

Here are some experiments related to tropical rain forests. You can do them in 20 minutes or less. If you need a science project by tomorrow, not much time is left. So let's get started!

1. Using Maps (20 minutes)

What's the Plan?

Let's find out where rain forests are located around the world. And let's find out in which type of biome you live.

WHAT YOU NEED:

- map of biomes in Figure 1
- map of the world or large world globe

What You Do

1. Examine the map in Figure 1. It shows where rain forests and other biomes are located.

2. Look at the places where rain forests are found. Compare them with the same places on a map of the world or on a world globe.

3. On which continents do you find rain forests? Are there any continents that do not have a rain forest?

4. Find where you live on a world map. Then, using Figure 1, find the biome where you live.

What's Going On?

You compared the map of biomes in Figure 1 with a map of the world. You could see that rain forests are not found in Europe or Antarctica. They exist on every other continent.

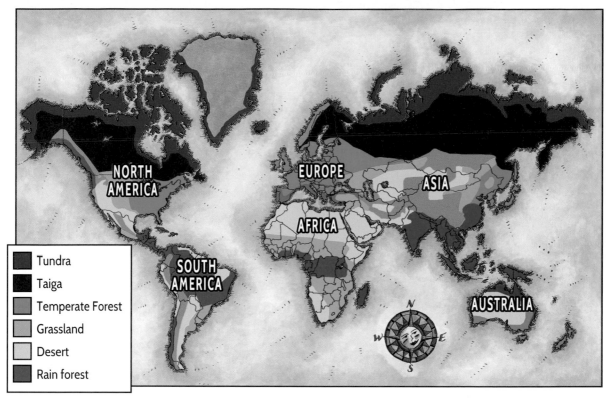

Tundra

Taiga

Temperate Forest

Grassland

Desert

Rain forest

Figure 1. The world's land biomes

By a similar comparison, you could see in which type of biome you live. Don't be surprised if you think the biome map for your home is wrong. The map shows what is true for much of the region where you live, not every part of it. For example, the author lives on Cape Cod in Massachusetts. The biome map indicates that he lives in a temperate forest biome. However, the outer end of Cape Cod is covered by sand dunes. Also, while forest covers much of Cape Cod, the trees are shorter than in a typical temperate forest. This is caused by the strong winds and salt air coming off the Atlantic Ocean.

2. A Climatogram of a City in a Rain Forest
(20 Minutes)

What's the Plan?

Let's make a climatogram for Manokwari, New Guinea. It is within a rain forest biome.

What You Do

1. Figure 2 shows what a climatogram looks like. Months of the year are plotted along the horizontal axis. Rainfall is plotted as a bar graph along the left vertical axis, and temperature is plotted as a line graph along the right vertical axis.

   Use a sheet of graph paper to make a climatogram for Manokwari. The climatogram will show Manokwari's average monthly temperature and rainfall. The data in Table 2 has the information you need. Use it to make the climatogram for Manokwari, New Guinea.

Table 2: Monthly average temperatures and rainfall for Manokwari, New Guinea												
	Jan.	Feb.	Mar.	Apr.	May	Jun.	Jul.	Aug.	Sept.	Oct.	Nov.	Dec.
Temp. (°C)	26.2	26.1	26.2	26.4	26.4	26.5	26.2	26.3	26.5	26.6	26.9	26.5
Rainfall (in.)	12.1	10.3	12.1	11.8	7.9	7.4	5.7	5.5	5.1	4.5	6.4	10.7

2. What is the approximate average temperature for one year in Manokwari?

3. What is the approximate total average rainfall for one year in Manokwari?

4. Are Manokwari's temperatures and rainfall normal for a rain forest? Does Manokwari have warm temperatures all year? Does it have at least 70 inches (180 cm) of rain?

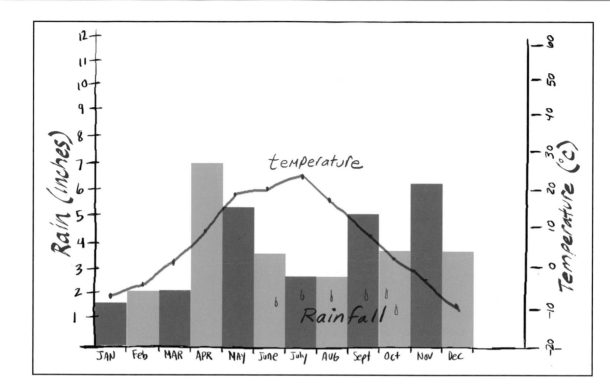

Figure 2. This is a sample climatogram. Now it is your turn to make one for Manokwari, New Guinea.

What's Going On?

Your climatogram should show Manokwari's average monthly temperature and rainfall in a graphical way. The approximate total annual precipitation in Manokwari is 99.5 inches. The approximate average annual temperature is 26.4°C (79.5°F). Its average monthly temperature varies by less than 0.5°C (0.9°F). These numbers are normal for a tropical rain forest where summer is the only season.

Keep Exploring–If You Have More Time!

• Prepare a climatogram of your city or town. What is your total yearly precipitation? Do you have cold winters and warm summers? What is your average annual temperature?

3. Buttress Roots: A Model
(20 minutes)

WHAT YOU NEED:

- an adult
- wood dowel about 9 in long with a diameter of ¾–1 in
- 3 thin, wood coffee stirrers
- sharp knife
- ruler
- clear tape

What's the Plan?

Trees in a temperate forest are supported by their deep roots. Many trees in a rain forest grow very tall. But rain forest trees cannot grow deep roots because the soil is shallow. Instead, many trees in a rain forest have what are called buttress roots. The photo below shows what buttress roots look like. To see how buttress roots strengthen a tall tree in a rain forest, you can make a model of a tree with buttress roots.

What You Do

1. Stand a wood dowel upright on a counter. Notice how easily it can be blown over. The dowel represents a rain forest tree without buttress roots.

2. Next, you'll need three thin coffee stirrers made of wood.

3. **Ask an adult** to use a sharp knife to score lines across each stirrer about 3/4 inch from each end (Figure 3a).

4. Bend the ends of each coffee stirrer along the scored lines. Do not break off the ends.

Buttress roots strengthen a tall tree in a rain forest.

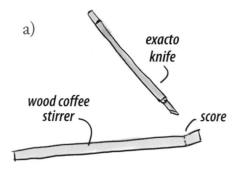

a)

exacto knife

wood coffee stirrer

score

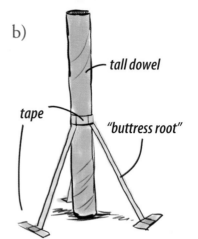

b)

tall dowel

tape

"buttress root"

Figure 3. Use a wood dowel and wood coffee stirrers to make a model of a rain forest tree with buttress roots.

5. Use clear tape to attach the bent end of a stirrer to the upright dowel. Do the same for the other two stirrers. Space the stirrers so they are separated by about one-third of the dowel's circumference. All three should be fastened at the same height.

6. Use short pieces of clear tape to fasten the free ends of the stirrers to the counter (Figure 3b). The pieces of tape represent the forest's soil. Is the dowel sturdier than it was without the "buttress roots?" Can you blow it over?

What's Going On?

The dowel represented a tall rain forest tree that could be easily blown over. Coffee stirrer buttress roots gave the "tree" much more stability and resistance to wind.

Keep Exploring–If You Have More Time!

- Using soda straws and pins, show that a diagonal is the best way to give a square structure stability.

- Stage a contest to see who can build the tallest tower using soda straws and pins.

4. Flying Frogs and Lizards (20 minutes)

What's the Plan?

In a rain forest, you'll find flying frogs and lizards. They don't really fly like birds. But they have skin that they can spread out by extending their legs and/or feet to become glider-like. This enables them to glide from tree to tree or limb to limb. (Lizards also extend their ribs. Their entire torso can act as an airfoil.) In North America, we have flying squirrels that can also glide. Let's make a model of a flying frog or lizard.

WHAT YOU NEED:

- **2 wood coffee stirrers**
- **clear tape or glue**
- **Figure 4**
- **sheet of paper**
- **ruler**
- **pen or pencil**
- **scissors**

What You Do

1. Tape or glue two wood coffee stirrers together as shown in Figure 4a.

2. Place the coffee stirrers on a sheet of paper (Figure 4b).

3. Use a ruler to draw the dotted lines shown in Figure 4b.

4. Use scissors to cut the paper along the dotted lines. Then attach the paper to the coffee stirrers using tape or glue.

5. If you used glue, wait for the glue to dry. Then release the "flying animal" as shown in Figure 4c. Watch its downward glide to the floor.

Wallace's flying frog (top) can glide from tree to tree. In North America, a Southern flying squirrel can glide as well.

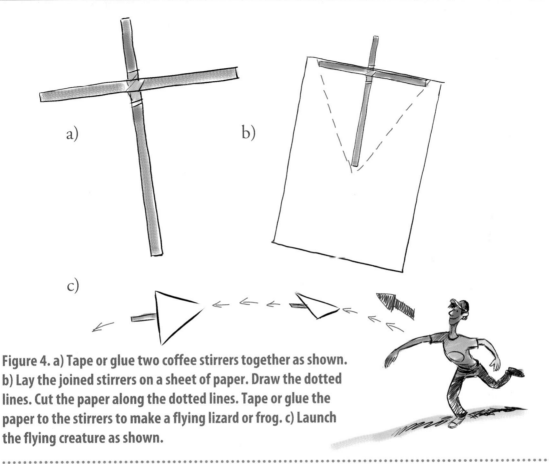

a)

b)

c)

Figure 4. a) Tape or glue two coffee stirrers together as shown. b) Lay the joined stirrers on a sheet of paper. Draw the dotted lines. Cut the paper along the dotted lines. Tape or glue the paper to the stirrers to make a flying lizard or frog. c) Launch the flying creature as shown.

What's Going On?

The paper wing provides the "animal" with lift. The body or wings act as an airfoil to keep the animal in the air while moving forward. That allows it to glide, not fall, downward.

Keep Exploring–If You Have More Time!

- Hold a contest with friends or classmates to see who can make a paper airplane fly the farthest.

- Using paper coffee filters, find out how surface area affects the rate at which the coffee filters fall.

5. Making a Cloud (20 minutes)

What's the Plan?

Clouds form almost every day above a rain forest. Let's make a cloud.

What You Do

1. Remove any paper from a clear, empty 2-liter plastic soda bottle.

2. Pour about half a cup of warm water into the bottle. Screw on the cap and shake the bottle vigorously. This will saturate the air inside with water vapor.

3. Hold the bottle up against a light background such as a window. Shake the bottle again. Then squeeze and release it. You will probably not see a cloud because one ingredient is missing—condensation nuclei. Condensation nuclei are the particles on which water vapor condenses to form the tiny droplets that make a cloud.

4. **Ask an adult** to light a match, blow it out, and quickly lower the match into the mouth of the bottle so that smoke particles (condensation nuclei) are inside the bottle.

5. Put the cap back on and again shake the bottle. Hold it up against a light background. Then squeeze it to increase the pressure inside the bottle. Quickly release your squeeze, decreasing the pressure inside the bottle. You should see a cloud form.

What's Going On?

The missing ingredient was the tiny particles of smoke, called condensation nuclei. Water vapor can cool to −40°C without condensing to liquid unless condensation nuclei are present. The molecules of water collect on the tiny particles, forming microscopic droplets. Clouds are made of these droplets. As the droplets collide, they may combine, grow larger, and eventually fall to the ground as raindrops. Each raindrop may consist of as many as a million cloud droplets.

Keep Exploring–If You Have More Time!

- Design and carry out an experiment to measure the size of raindrops. Does the size of the drops change as a storm progresses? Warning! Do not do this experiment during a thunderstorm.

6. Camouflage: Present but Out-of-Sight (30 Minutes)

What's the Plan?

Many animals in a rain forest use camouflage to avoid predators. Their color matches their surroundings or they resemble some inedible object such as a stick. Let's do an experiment to see how camouflage can keep a predator from finding its prey.

What You Do

1. Mix together about 100 red and 100 green toothpicks.

2. Spread the toothpicks on a square section of green lawn about 10 meters (yards) on a side. Or spread 50 toothpicks of each color over a very large green rug.

3. Consider the toothpicks to be the "prey." Ask a partner, who did not see you spread the toothpicks, to be the "predator." As predator, he or she will seek the toothpick prey.

4. After two minutes, collect the toothpicks the predator has found. Do the same after four minutes and after six minutes. Keep the two, four, and six minute piles separate.

WHAT YOU NEED:

- **100 red and 100 green toothpicks (from a supermarket or novelty store)**
- **green lawn or large green rug**
- **a partner**
- **clock or watch**

5. Count the number of red and green toothpicks in each pile. What can you conclude?

What's Going On?

You probably found that initially the predator found many more red than green prey. The green prey were protected by camouflage like the tree frog in the photograph. The green prey blended with their green surroundings. The red were more easily seen because their color contrasted with the green grass or rug.

Keep Exploring—If You Have More Time!

- Look for animals that exhibit camouflage. For example, look for insects such as a grasshopper, walking stick, or praying mantis.

This tree frog blends in well with its environment.

7. Finding a Dew Point and Humidity (30 Minutes)

WHAT YOU NEED:
- warm water
- shiny metal can (a clean, empty tin can will do)
- thermometer
- ice

What's the Plan?

A dew point is the temperature at which water vapor in the air begins to condense and form dew. It's the temperature at which the air can hold no more water vapor. Rain forests have very high dew points. Let's measure the dew point in your home or school.

What You Do

1. Pour some warm water into a shiny metal can. Stir the water carefully with a thermometer. If no dew forms on the can's surface, go to step 2. If dew does form, replace the warm water with very hot water before continuing.

2. Slowly lower the water temperature by adding small pieces of ice.

3. Watch the surface of the can closely. When tiny dew droplets are seen on the can's shiny surface, note the temperature of the water. You've reached the dew point of the air.

Dew drops form on a rain forest leaf.

24

Table 3: The maximum mass of water vapor found in a cubic meter of air at different temperatures					
Temperature			Temperature		
(°C)	(°F)	Grams of water per m^3	(°C)	(°F)	Grams of water per m^3
0	32	4.8	20	68	17.1
5	41	6.8	25	77	22.8
10	50	9.3	30	86	30.0
15	59	12.7	35	95	39.2

What's Going On?

When water evaporates, it becomes a gas. It mixes with the other gases (mostly nitrogen and oxygen) in the air. By measuring the dew point, you can find the mass of water vapor in a cubic meter (m^3) of the air (see Table 3). The dew point is the temperature at which the air can hold no additional water vapor. At the dew point, moisture in the air begins to condense on surfaces, forming tiny water droplets. As Table 3 shows, the warmer the air, the more water vapor it can hold.

Figure 5 is a graph of the data in Table 3. The graph will help you determine values for humidity at temperatures between those in the table.

You can use your experimental data and Figure 5 to find what is called the absolute humidity. Suppose dew appears when the water and can are at 10°C (50°F). From Table 3 or Figure 5, you then know that the air touching the can contains 9.3 g/m^3—the maximum amount of water vapor air can hold at 10°C. The absolute humidity of this air is 9.3 g/m^3; that is, 9.3 grams of water vapor per cubic meter of air.

The relative humidity of air is the ratio of the quantity of water vapor the air *does* hold to the quantity it *could* hold at air temperature. If the air temperature

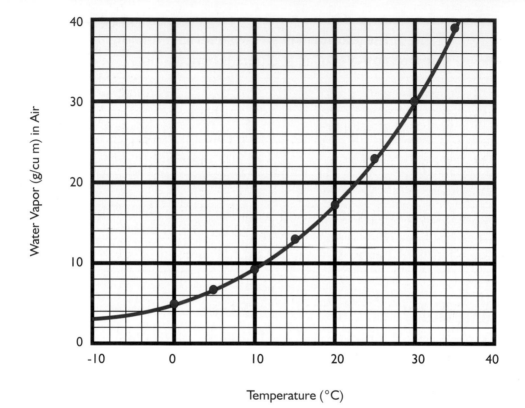

Figure 5. A graph showing grams of water vapor per cubic meter of air versus air temperature in degrees Celsius.

is 20°C (68°F), the air could hold 17.1 g/m³. Consequently, the relative humidity of the air is 9.3 ÷ 17.1, which equals 0.54 or 54 percent.

What is the relative humidity of the air in your experiment?

In a rain forest, the relative humidity is usually very close to 100 percent. When it is raining, the relative humidity is 100 percent. A rain forest is a very hot and humid place.

Keep Exploring–If You Have More Time!

- Design and carry out an experiment to show why you should use a shiny metal rather than a plastic or glass container to find dew points.

- You will often find dew on grass and flowers after a cool, clear night. Why is dew less likely if clouds cover the sky?

- Using the same apparatus, table, and graph, determine the dew point and humidity (absolute and relative) on clear, cloudy, and rainy days, and at different times of the year. Record your findings. During which season is the absolute humidity highest? Lowest? When is the relative humidity highest? Lowest? During which season is the air driest inside your home or school? Under what conditions are you unable to determine the dew point?

- Fill the metal can you used about one-third of the way with crushed ice. Add an equal volume of table salt and stir to thoroughly mix the salt and ice. Place a thermometer in the salt-ice mixture. Watch the side of the can very carefully. Do you see frost collecting? Do you first see dew that then freezes, or does the frost form without first forming dew?

8. How Long Will Rain Forests Exist?
(30 minutes)

What's the Plan?

Rain forests once covered 14 percent of the world's land. They now cover half that amount. Water covers 70 percent of the earth's 200 million square miles of surface. Only 60 million square miles are dry land. Only seven percent of that land (4.2 million square miles) is rain forest. Let's estimate how long rain forests will exist if they continue to be destroyed at current rates.

What You Do

Estimates on the rate at which rain forests are being deforested vary. One of the higher estimates is 78 million acres per year; a lower estimate is 34 million acres per year.

1. Based on the higher estimate, how many years will it be before rain forests no longer exist? (Hint: There are 640 acres in a square mile.)

2. Based on the lower estimate, how many years will it be before rain forests no longer exist?

What's Going On?

To convert acres to square miles (mi^2), you need to divide by 640 because there are 640 acres in a square mile. Dividing 78,000,000 acres/year by 640 acres/mi^2 gives approximately 122,000 mi^2/year. Then, 4,200,000 mi^2 divided by 122,000 mi^2/year equals about 34 years.

Show that the lower estimate of the rate of rain forest destruction gives rain forests about 79 more years of existence.

Rain forest destruction in Thailand

Keep Exploring—If You Have More Time!

- How is the rate of deforestation of rain forests measured?

- The world's population is expected to increase from seven billion to nine billion by 2050. How might this affect the rate at which rain forests will disappear?

- What can be done to save rain forests, which are often called Earth's lungs?

9. The Tropical Sun Over Rain Forests (30 minutes)

WHAT YOU NEED:
- world globe
- large empty tin can
- bright sunlight
- scissors
- drinking straw
- pin

What's the Plan?

Let's see why tropical rain forests are always warm.

What You Do

1. Find a globe that is at least 30 cm (12 in) in diameter. Remove it from its stand. Place it on a large empty tin can in bright sunlight.

2. Turn the globe so that the town where you live is at the top of the globe—the way you see Earth.

3. Turn the globe so that its North Pole is turned toward the north. (If you need help with the direction, ask an adult.)

4. You have made a global model of Earth that has the same orientation to the sun. You can find where the sun is directly overhead right now. Cut off a short length of a straw. Stick a pin through it. Move the straw along the globe near the equator. Keep it perpendicular to the globe's surface. Find a place where the sun shines straight through the straw and casts no shadow (Figure 6). At this place, the sun must be directly overhead.

5. Move the straw north along the longitude line until you are north of the Tropic of Cancer. Keeping it perpendicular to the globe, observe the straw's shadow length here.

6. Move the straw southward along the same longitude line until you are south of the Tropic of Capricorn. Observe the straw's shadow length here.

30

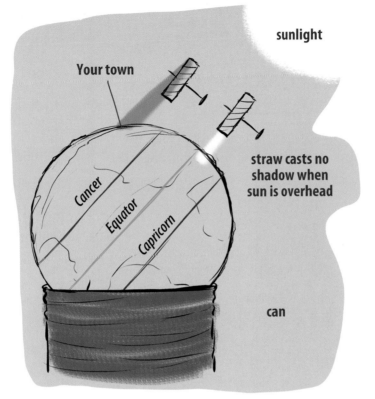

sunlight

Your town

straw casts no
shadow when
sun is overhead

Cancer

Equator

Capricorn

can

Figure 6. Using a globe, you can find where the sun is overhead right now.

7. Finally, move the straw along the same longitude line to the latitude where you live. Compare its shadow length here with its length at the tropics of Cancer and Capricorn.

What's Going On?

The tropics lie between the tropics of Cancer and Capricorn, as do the rain forests. The sun is always directly overhead somewhere in the tropics, never elsewhere. You saw that shadows in the tropics are quite short compared to shadows where you probably live. This means the tropical sun is high in the sky there. The sun's altitude in the tropics is higher than in other places on earth. A high sun provides lots of heat, so the tropics are warm all year.

10. What Does an Acre Look Like? (1 hour)

WHAT YOU NEED:

- large field
- 4 small wooden stakes
- hammer
- long measuring tape
- plenty of string (optional)

What's the Plan?

According to one estimate, the world's rain forests are disappearing at a rate of 34 million acres per year or about one acre per second. Let's find out what an acre looks like.

What You Do

An acre is 43,560 square feet (ft^2) or 160 square rods. (A rod is a length of 5.5 yards or 16.5 feet.)

1. To see what an acre looks like, go to a large field.

2. At a corner of the field, drive a small stake into the ground. Starting from that stake, measure a straight line 209 feet long. Drive another stake at the end of that line.

3. Measure another line 209 feet long that is perpendicular to the end of the first line.

4. Two more lines at right angles to the first lines (Figure 7) will enclose an area that is slightly more than one acre.

5. If you have time, and plenty of string, you could enclose your acre with string connected to all four stakes.

6. Remove the stakes and string.

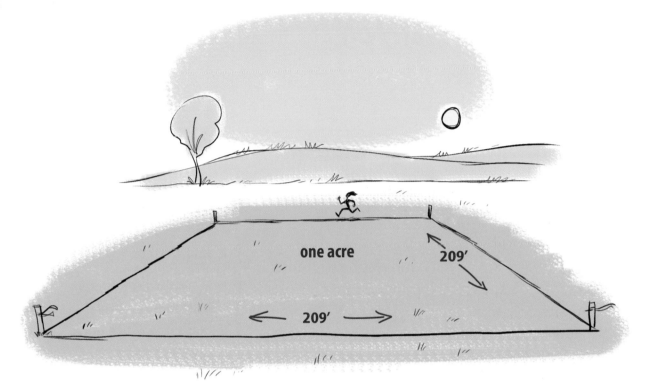

Figure 7. The diagram shows an area slightly larger than one acre.

What's Going On?

Since an acre is 43,560 square feet, an acre that is a square would be 208.71033 feet on a side (the square root of 43,560 square feet). The square you laid out is slightly larger, but it gives you a pretty good sense of what an acre looks like. Now, imagine that much area of rain forest disappearing every second.

Keep Exploring–If You Have More Time!

- Land area is also measured in hectares. A hectare is 10,000 square meters. How many acres are there in one hectare?

- How large is your school's playground in square feet? In acres? In hectares?

Two Hours or More

2 hours or more

Are you a budding scientist with some more time on your hands? The next experiments take at least two hours, but it will be time well spent!

11. Animal Size: An Adaptation to the Rain Forest (2 hours)

What's the Plan?

In the rain forest you may find elephants, buffalo, deer, wild pigs, pygmy hippopotamuses, pygmy chimpanzees, even human pygmies. *Pygmy* is the key word. Rain forest animals are smaller than similar animals found on a grassland. Their reduced size allows them to move more easily between the closely spaced trees. But let's see if reduced size offers another advantage to life in the warm, humid rain forest.

What You Do

1. Using soft clay and a metric ruler, make a cube that is 1 centimeter (cm) on a side (Figure 8a). What is the volume of the cube in cubic centimeters (cm^3)? What is the total surface area of the cube in square centimeters (cm^2)?

2. Next, make a cube that is 2 centimeters on a side (Figure 8b). What is the volume of this cube? What is the total surface area of this cube?

A pygmy hippo from the rain forest (shown left with its baby) is half the height of a grassland hippo (below).

3. What would be the volume and total surface area of a cube 10 centimeters on a side?

4. For each cube you made, what is the ratio of the cube's surface area to its volume? What is the ratio of surface area to volume for a cube 10 cm on a side?

How might smaller animal size be an advantage in a warm rain forest?

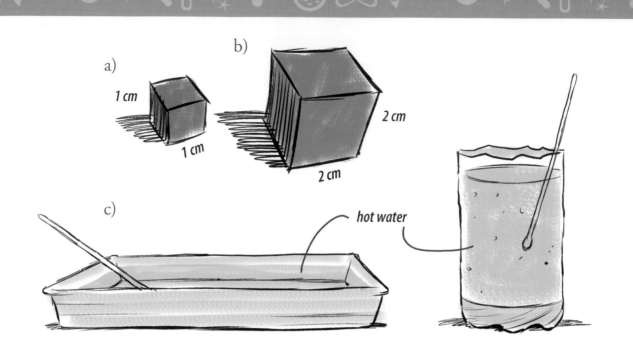

a)

1 cm

1 cm

b)

2 cm

2 cm

c)

hot water

wide, shallow container

tall, narrow container

Figure 8. a) Make a clay cube 1 cm on a side. b) Make a clay cube 2 cm on a side. c) Two containers that will hold two equal volumes of hot water with different surface areas exposed to cooler air.

What's Going On?

A cube 1.0 cm on a side has a volume of 1.0 cm^3 (1 cm x 1 cm x 1 cm). The cube has six sides and each side has a surface area of 1.0 cm^2 (1.0 cm x 1.0 cm) so the total surface area is 6 cm^2. Its surface area to volume ratio is 6 cm^2/1.0 cm^3 = a numerical ratio of 6:1.

A cube 2.0 cm on a side has a volume of 8 cm^3 (2 cm x 2 cm x 2 cm). The cube has six sides and each side has a surface area of 4 cm^2 (2 cm x 2 cm) so the total surface area is 24 cm^2. Its surface area to volume ratio is 24 cm^2/ 8.0 cm^3 = a numerical ratio of 3:1.

A cube 10 cm on a side has a volume of 1,000 cm^3 (10 cm x 10 cm x 10 cm). The cube's six sides each have a surface area of 100 cm^2 (10 cm x 10 cm) so the total surface area is 600 cm^2. Its surface area to volume ratio is 600 cm^2/1,000 cm^3 = a numerical ratio of 0.6:1.

As you have found, the smaller the cube, the larger its surface area to volume ratio. The same is true of animals. Small animals have a bigger surface area to volume ratio than large animals.

An animal loses heat through its surface. A small animal has more surface per volume than a large animal of the same shape. So being smaller in a rain forest allows a smaller elephant to lose heat faster than a big elephant. The same is true of other rain forest animals as well.

What's the Plan?

Let's do an experiment to show that a larger surface area to volume ratio really does cause heat to be lost faster.

What You Do

1. Find two plastic containers. One should be shallow and wide. The other should be taller and less wide (Figure 8c).

2. Add one cup of hot water to each of the two plastic containers. In which container does the water have more surface area?

3. Use a thermometer to measure the water temperature in each container at ten minute intervals. (To speed up heat loss, place the containers in a cool place.)

   In which container does the water cool faster? What can you conclude?

What's Going On?

You probably found that the water with more surface exposed to the cooler air cooled faster. Heat is lost through surface touching cooler air. The more surface, the faster heat is lost. Small animals have an advantage in a warm climate where shedding heat is necessary to avoid excessive body warmth. In a cold climate, small animals are at a disadvantage. They may not be able to eat enough food to supply the body heat they need to stay warm.

12. The Water Cycle: A Major Cycle in a Rain Forest
(2 hours)

WHAT YOU NEED:

- large, clear plastic box, or a shoe box and plastic wrap
- green leaves
- warm water
- warm sunlight or a heat lamp
- plastic wrap
- tape or large rubber band
- ice cubes

What's the Plan?

Let's make a model of the water cycle that occurs almost daily in a rain forest.

What You Do

1. Obtain a large, clear plastic box. Or line a shoe box with a sheet of plastic wrap.

2. Put some green leaves in the box to represent the plants in a rain forest.

3. Add an inch or two of warm water to the bottom of the box. The water represents the large amount of moisture that exists in a rain forest. Replace the cover or cover the top of the box with plastic wrap. Seal the cover with tape (Figure 9). Add a few ice cubes to the cover to represent the cooling that occurs when water vapor rises into the air.

4. Place the box in bright, warm sunlight or under a heat lamp that represents the sun.

5. Observe the box every few minutes for an hour or two. Can you see drops forming on the plastic cover? Where do you think that water came from? What must have happened?

   Do any of the droplets grow large enough to "rain" on the "forest" below?

sunlight

plastic wrap

ice cubes

rubber band

water droplets

warm water and leaves

Figure 9. You can make a model of the water cycle.

What's Going On?

Heat from the sun or heat lamp warms the water just as the tropical sun warms a rain forest. Some of the water evaporates (changes to a gas). As the gaseous water cools, it condenses back to liquid water on the plastic cover. The cover represents the cooler air above the rain forest. The drops that form may grow large enough to fall as "rain."

The water cycle exists on a global scale. Earth's annual rainfall equals the amount of water (122,000 cubic miles) that evaporates from Earth's land to its atmosphere.

Keep Exploring—If You Have More Time!

• Under adult supervision, you can do a similar experiment to model the water cycle. Wearing gloves, hold a pan of ice water above steam coming from a tea kettle. Can you make it "rain?"

13. How Raindrops Form
(2 hours)

WHAT YOU NEED:

- **wide, clear plastic container that can be sealed**
- **2 metal jar lids**
- **warm water**
- **table salt crystals**
- **cover or plastic wrap and tape**

What's the Plan?

Let's do an experiment to see how raindrops form in clouds over a rain forest.

What You Do

1. Find a wide, clear plastic container that can be sealed. Put a metal jar lid, open side down, on the bottom of the container (see Figure 10a).

2. Cover the bottom of the container with a shallow layer of warm water. The water should not cover the jar lid.

3. Hold a second metal jar lid open side up. Add a few crystals of table salt to the second metal jar lid. Place the second lid on the first one as shown in Figure 10b.

4. Seal the plastic container by adding its cover or taping plastic wrap over it. The warm water will evaporate, filling the container with water vapor.

5. Examine the salt crystals every 15 minutes. What happens to the crystals?

6. Do "raindrops" form? If drops have formed and the air outside the container is very dry, remove the lid. Watch the "raindrops." Do they evaporate, leaving the solid salt crystals?

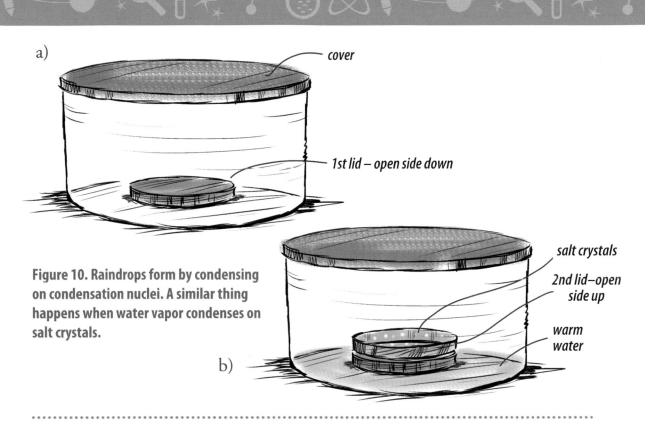

a)

cover

1st lid – open side down

salt crystals

2nd lid–open side up

warm water

b)

Figure 10. Raindrops form by condensing on condensation nuclei. A similar thing happens when water vapor condenses on salt crystals.

What's Going On?

As water vapor is carried up into the atmosphere, the gas expands because air pressure decreases with altitude. When any gas expands, it cools, so its temperature decreases. The cooler water molecules move slower. Their slower speed makes it possible for them to come together and condense back to a liquid. However, these molecules may or may not come together to form clouds, which consist of tiny water droplets. For raindrops to form, more is needed than cold temperatures. There must be tiny particles on which the gaseous water molecules can condense. These particles are known as condensation nuclei. Without condensation nuclei, water vapor can cool to temperatures as low as –40°C (–40°F) without condensing.

Tiny salt crystals and other particles in the air commonly serve as condensation nuclei. These particles are truly tiny. They are about one tenth of a micron (0.00001 cm).

14. How Plants Seek Light
(1 or 2 weeks)

WHAT YOU NEED:

- sunlight
- leafy potted plant
- south–facing window
- water

What's the Plan?

In a rain forest many plants compete for the limited light that comes through the taller trees. Let's see how plants seek the best light available.

What You Do

Green plants, in a process called photosynthesis, combine carbon dioxide and water to make sugar, which they use for energy. For this to happen, the plants need sunlight.

1. Place a leafy potted plant near a south-facing window where the sun shines in most of the day. The plant's leaves should be turned in all directions or turned predominantly toward the darker side of the room.

2. Keep the soil in the pot damp but not wet.

3. Examine the plant daily over a period of a week or two. What happens to the leaves? Do they turn toward the light? What does this tell you about one way green plants have adapted to their environment?

What's Going On?

Plants need light to survive. One way they have adapted to this need is to turn toward light. Light provides the energy they need to make food. This turning toward light is known as phototropism. Plant cells contain a hormone that causes phototropism. Light shining on one side of a plant's stem causes many of these hormone molecules to move to cells on the darker side of the stem. Once there, the hormone causes those cells to grow longer. This causes the leaf to turn toward the light.

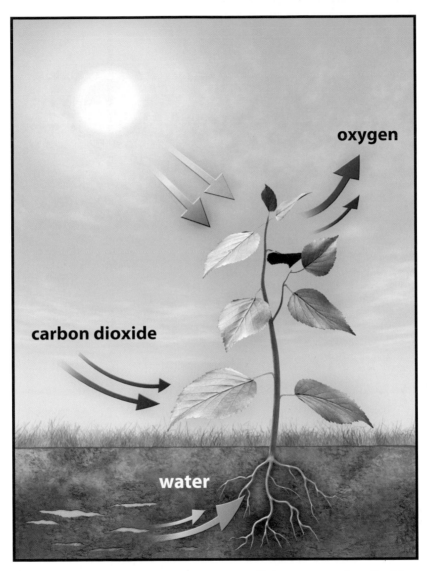

During photosynthesis, green plants use sunlight to turn carbon dioxide and water into sugar. They use the sugar for energy and give off oxygen.

Keep Exploring—If You Have More Time!

- Under adult supervision, design and do an experiment to show that plant leaves manufacture food when exposed to sunlight.

15. How Does Your Rainfall Compare with a Rain Forest? (1 month or more)

WHAT YOU NEED:

- an adult
- clear glass or plastic jar with straight sides such as an olive jar
- ruler and masking tape, or ruled tape
- stake and duct tape (optional)
- pen or pencil
- notebook
- local newspaper

What's the Plan?

Let's measure your rainfall and see how it compares with rainfall in a rain forest.

What You Do

Rain is measured by the depth of the water it produces.

1. If you don't have a rain gauge, you can make one. Find a clear glass or plastic jar with straight sides. An olive jar works well. Put a strip of centimeter tape on the side of the jar. Or place a strip of narrow masking tape on the jar. Mark the tape with lines 0.5 cm or ¼ in apart (Figure 11).

2. Place the jar in an open area away from buildings and trees. You might tape the jar to a stake.

3. After a rainfall, measure the depth of the water in the jar.

4. After measuring a rainfall, record the measurement, empty the jar, and replace it. You might compare your rainfall measurement with one published in your local newspaper or TV station. Be sure to check the gauge every morning. It may have rained during the night.

5. Measure rainfall for at least one month. Record the rainfall each time it rains. At the end of the month, add your numbers to find the total for the month.

The average monthly rainfall in a rain forest would be at least 15 cm (6 inches), probably more. How does your rainfall compare with that in a rain forest? Of course, a better way to compare would be to record rainfall for more than one month.

What's Going On?

Unless you had a very rainy month, you probably found your rainfall was much less than rainfall in a typical rain forest.

Keep Exploring–If You Have More Time!

• Find a way to convert the inches of snow that falls during a snowstorm to inches of rain.

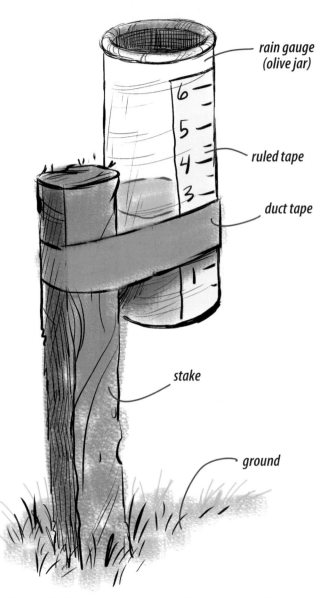

Figure 11. You can make a gauge to measure rain.

45

Words to Know

acre—An area of land equal to 43,560 square feet, 4,840 square yards, or 0.405 hectare.

biome—A region of the earth with a characteristic climate and species of plants and animals.

buttress roots—Roots that arise from the trunk of a tree and, like a building's buttressed wall, strengthen a tall tree.

camouflage—An animal's coloring or structure that allows it to blend in with its surroundings.

cloud—A cloud consists of tiny droplets of water. Droplets may collide, join, grow larger, and eventually fall to the ground as raindrops.

dew point—The temperature at which the air can hold no additional water vapor. At the dew point, moisture in the air begins to condense on surfaces, forming tiny water droplets.

hectare—An area of land equal to 10,000 square meters or 2.471 acres.

phototropism—A plant's tendency to turn toward light.

relative humidity—The ratio of the quantity of water vapor the air does hold to the quantity it could hold at the temperature of the air.

Tropic of Cancer—An imaginary line that goes around Earth 23.5 degrees north of the equator. The sun is directly above this latitude on the first day of summer in the Northern Hemisphere.

Tropic of Capricorn—An imaginary line that goes around Earth 23.5 degrees south of the equator. The sun is directly above this latitude on the first day of winter in the Northern Hemisphere.

Further Reading

Bardhan-Quallen, Sudipta. *Championship Science Fair Projects: 100 Sure-to-Win Experiments.* New York: Sterling, 2005.

Benoit, Peter. *Tropical Rain Forests.* New York: Children's Press, 2011.

Hamilton, Jean. *The Secrets of Tropical Rain Forests: Hot and Humid and Teeming with Life.* Montrose, Calif.: London Town Press, 2005.

Morgan, Sally. *Rain Forests in Danger.* Mankato, Minn.: Sea-to-Sea Publications, 2010.

Newland, Sonya. *Rain Forest Animals.* Mankato, Minn.: Smart Apple Media, 2012.

Rhatigan, Joe, and Rain Newcomb. *Prize-Winning Science Fair Projects for Curious Kids.* New York: Lark Books, 2006.

Simon, Seymour. *Tropical Rain Forests.* Washington, D.C.: HarperCollins, 2010.

Taylor, Barbara. *Hidden in the Trees.* Mankato, Minn.: QEB Publications, 2011.

Internet Addresses

Rainforest Facts

<http://www.rain-tree.com/facts.htm>

World Biomes—Kids Do Ecology

<http://kids.nceas.ucsb.edu/biomes/index.html>

Index